STAR WARS™
Grogu's Galaxy

DK
Senior Editor Matt Jones
Project Art Editor Chris Gould
Production Editor Marc Staples
Senior Production Controller Mary Slater
Managing Editor Emma Grange
Managing Art Editor Vicky Short
Publishing Director Mark Searle

Designed for DK by Sandra Perry
Reading Consultant Barbara Marinak

For Lucasfilm
Senior Editor Brett Rector
Creative Director, Publishing
Michael Siglain
Art Director Troy Alders
Story Group Leland Chee, Pablo Hidalgo,
and Kate Izquierdo
Creative Art Manager Phil Szostak

Asset Management Sarah Williams,
Elinor De La Torre, Jackey Cabrera, Bryce
Pinkos, Erik Sanchez, and Shahana Alam

DK would like to thank Chelsea Alon and
Krista Wong at Disney; and Julia March and
Megan Douglass for proofreading.

First American Edition, 2023
Published in the United States by
DK Publishing
1745 Broadway, 20th Floor, New York,
NY 10019

Page design copyright © 2023
Dorling Kindersley Limited
DK, a Division of Penguin
Random House LLC

A catalog record for this book
is available from the Library of Congress.
ISBN 978-0-7440-7065-1 (Paperback)
ISBN 978-0-7440-7066-8 (Hardcover)

DK books are available at special discounts when purchased
in bulk for sales promotions, premiums, fund-raising, or educational use.
For details, contact: DK Publishing Special Markets,
1745 Broadway, 20th Floor, New York, NY 10019
SpecialSales@dk.com

Printed and bound in China

For the curious

www.dk.com
www.starwars.com

MIX
Paper | Supporting
responsible forestry
FSC
www.fsc.org FSC™ C018179

This book was made with Forest
Stewardship Council ™ certified
paper—one small step in DK's
commitment to a sustainable future.
For more information go to
www.dk.com/our-green-pledge

STAR WARS™
Grogu's Galaxy

Matt Jones

Contents

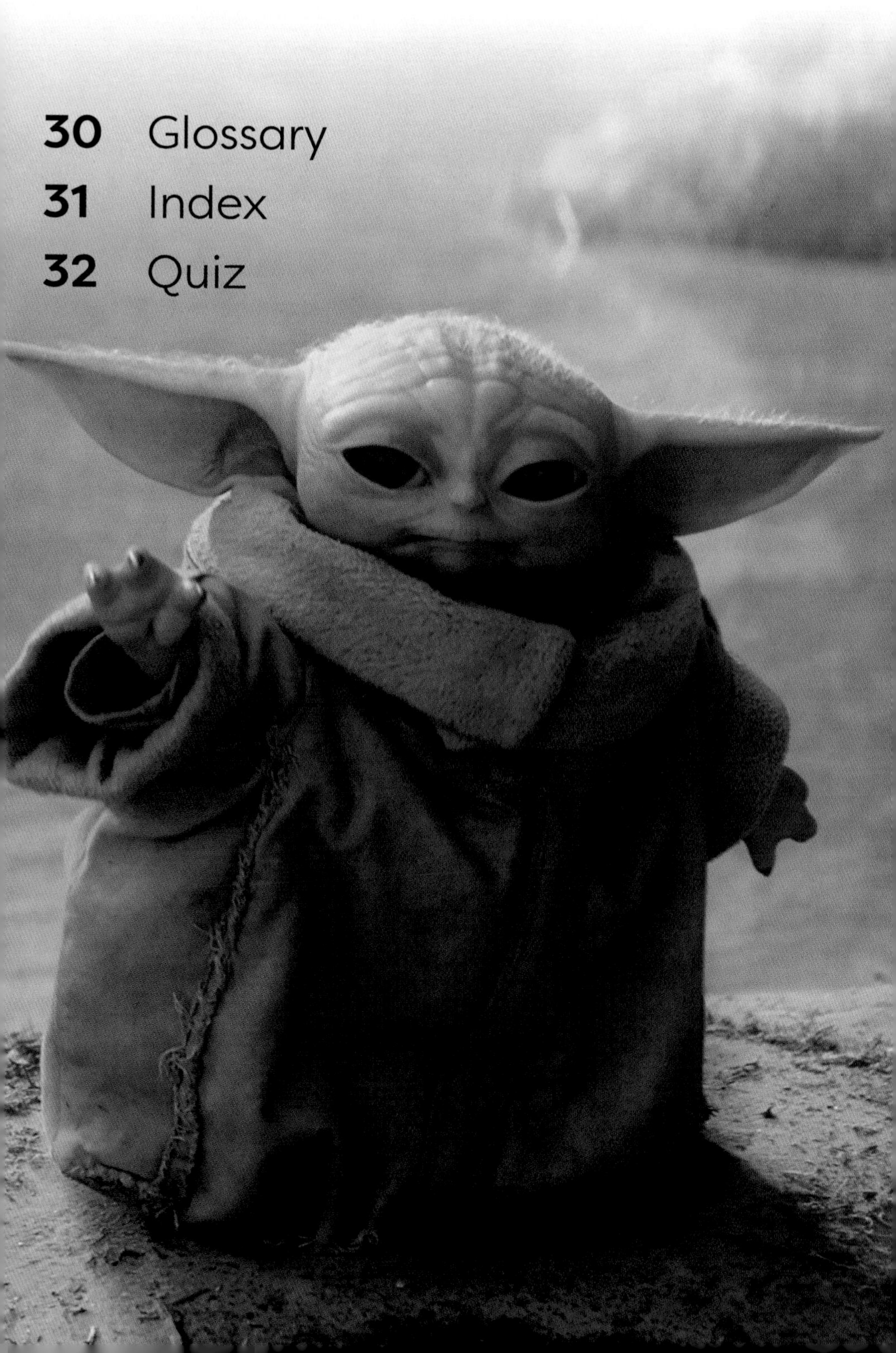

Grogu

Say hello to Grogu. Grogu is from another galaxy.

Grogu cares about
his friends.

Grogu's friend

The Mandalorian

The Mandalorian is called Din Djarin.
He is Grogu's friend.

Din keeps Grogu safe.

The Force

The Force is a powerful energy. Some people use the Force to do great things.

Grogu and the Force

Grogu can use the Force. He can use it to put creatures to sleep.

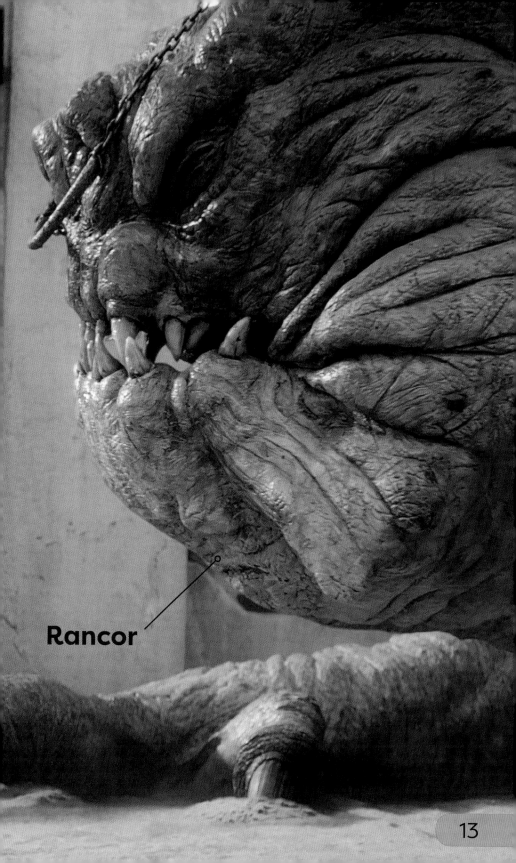

Rancor

Kuiil

Kuiil lives on the planet Arvala-7. He likes to fix machines.

Kuiil helps Din and Grogu
to repair their starship.

Grogu's pram

Grogu has a special pram.
It can float in the air.

His friend Kuiil made it for him.

Peli Motto

Peli Motto is one of Grogu's friends. She loves taking care of Grogu.

Grogu and Peli have lots of fun together.

Hungry Grogu

Grogu gets hungry very often.
He likes to try different types of food.

Soup

Squid

Cookie

Spider eggs

Ahsoka Tano

Ahsoka Tano is
a smart hero.

She can use the Force.
Grogu meets Ahsoka on
the planet Corvus.

Zooming ship

Grogu enjoys it when starships move really fast.

He gets very
excited.

Zoom!

Luke Skywalker

Luke Skywalker is a Jedi.
Jedi can use the Force
to help people.
Luke teaches Grogu
about the Force.

Great team

Grogu and Din are
a great team.
They visit many
planets together.

Glossary

 **galaxy**
a large group of stars and planets

 **pram**
another word for a baby carriage

 **rancor**
a type of creature

 **repair**
mending something that is broken

 **starship**
a type of ship used to travel in space

Index

Quiz

Ready to find out how much you have learned? Read the questions and then check your answers with an adult.

1. Is Luke Skywalker a Jedi?
2. Who repairs Din and Grogu's starship?
3. Where does Ahsoka Tano meet Grogu?
4. What is the Mandalorian's name?
5. Can Grogu use the Force?

1. Yes 2. Kuiil 3. The planet Corvus 4. Din Djarin 5. Yes